CW00376885

The Story of Titania and Oberon

For Hattie, Billy, George, Alfie, Dominic, Grace, Emmeline, Mariella and others

First published in the UK in 1945 by Peter Lunn (Publishers) Ltd

This edition published in the United Kingdom in 2017 by
Pavilion Books Company Limited
43 Great Ormond Street
London WC1N 3HZ

About the illustrator text © David Buckman 2017

All rights reserved. No part of this publication may be reproduced,
stored in a retrieval system, or transmitted in any form or by any means
electronic, mechanical, photocopying, recording or otherwise, without
prior permission of the copyright owner.

ISBN: 9781843653295

A CIP catalogue record for this book is available from the British Library.

10 9 8 7 6 5 4 3 2 1

Reproduction by Mission Productions, Hong Kong
Printed by Toppan Leefung Printing Ltd, China

This book can be ordered directly from the publisher online
at www.pavilionbooks.com, or try your local bookshop.

Every effort has been made to trace copyright holders and to obtain their
permission for the use of copyright material. The publisher would be grateful
if notified of any corrections that should be incorporated in future reprints or
editions of this book.

MIX
Paper from
responsible sources
FSC
www.fsc.org
FSC® C104723

The Story of Titania and Oberon

from *A Mid-summer Night's Dream*
by Shakespeare

illustrated by

Phyllis Bray

told by

Jo Manton

About the illustrator, Phyllis Bray

The illustrator of this book, Phyllis Bray, was a hugely versatile artist over many years. Whereas some artists when young adopt a subject or medium and stick to it throughout their careers – such as painting just portraits or concentrating only on the printed page – Bray always relished a new challenge. This became evident in 2005 when a posthumous Bray studio sale was held in London's West End. The hundreds of items on offer reflected an output that had included designs for bookplates, sweet wrappers, paper bags and glass engravings; over 200 landscape gouaches; plus oil paintings. She also had the ability to tackle big projects, such as murals in churches and public buildings.

Bray's engagement with book illustration began in her mid-twenties. Periodically over the next two decades she would complete commissions for major publishers including Faber & Faber, J M Dent and Sons and the Oxford University Press. In 1935 she designed the jacket for *The Children's Book of Holiday Verse*, followed in 1936 by her striking cover for Elizabeth Garner's *Duet in Discord*. This was followed in 1938 by illustrations for Arthur Stanley's *The Golden Road: An Anthology of Travel*, then in the next year she illustrated a book of Charles Dickens' *The Magic Fishbone* and *The King of the Golden River*, by John Ruskin, as well as the well-known children's author Alison Uttley's *A Traveller in Time* (republished in America in 2011). In 1945 came Rhoda Power's *Here and There Stories*, and the title you're holding, Jo Manton's *The Story of Titania and Oberon* (republished in 1953); designs for Michael Fyodrov's *Matushka* in 1946; and Jo (as Joan Granville) Manton's *The Enchanted Ship and Other Greek Legends*, in 1950.

This edition of *Titania and Oberon* uses the original artwork for the story. The cover also reproduces the original art, although since publication letters have come to light between Bray and her publisher, debating the colour used as a background. Apparently the artist was not happy with the colour originally chosen (deep red). With this in mind, this edition uses one of Bray's more favoured colours (a purple/blue) on the cover.

Phyllis Bray was born on August 30, 1911, and, after studying at Queenwood, Eastbourne, attended the Slade School of Fine Art between 1927-31, where she was fortunate to catch the end of Henry Tonks' distinguished professorship. Bray was a gifted student and won a string of awards.

Bray gained her fine art diploma in 1931, and that summer married the charismatic John Cooper, who taught evening classes after he left the Slade in 1922. By 1931, Cooper had established the East London Group through classes he taught at the Bow & Bromley Evening Institute in Coborn Road. The Group consisted of mostly working class, realist painters with little formal education. The debut exhibition of work at the Whitechapel Art Gallery in December 1928, part of which was shown at what is now Tate Britain in early 1929, led in November of that year to the first of eight annual East London Group exhibitions at Alex Reid & Lefevre, patronised by wealthy, society collectors.

The show was an astonishing success and had to be extended for several weeks, described by the *Manchester Guardian* as "one of the most interesting and significant things in the London art season". It was there that Cooper and other East London Group stalwarts, including William Coldstream, Murroe FitzGerald, Archibald Hattemore, Elwin Hawthorne, Harold and Walter Steggles, and Albert Turpin established their careers.

Phyllis Bray began her participation by showing two paintings at the second exhibition in 1930, among a total of ninety catalogued works, and each year after that her paintings and drawings became important features of these group shows. She was also a valuable additional teacher at Bow. By the 1937-38 academic season, Bray took responsibility for overseeing the students, with the support of another teacher. By then her marriage to Cooper had collapsed.

In 1936 came Bray's commission to paint murals for the New People's Palace. The old People's Palace had long been a centre of East End cultural life. Its creation was due to the beneficence of painter, property owner and philanthropist John Barber Beaumont who donated money to found a Philosophical Institution in Mile End that would provide educational and recreational facilities for working men. In 1887, Queen Victoria opened the Queen's Hall as part of her Golden Jubilee celebrations but a fire had destroyed the building in 1931. Construction of a New People's Palace proceeded in 1936.

This was a huge commission for a young artist with no experience of working on such a scale. At the Queen's Hall, it was decided that Bray would undertake three panels on canvas, each twelve feet by ten feet, and the subjects would be The Dance, The Drama and Music.

Although the New People's Palace enjoyed some success before the war, by 1953 it was put up for sale and Queen Mary College acquired it. The fate of the murals was unknown until 2011 when the College began restoration work, and the mystery was uncovered. Although the lower half of the murals had been destroyed when the hall was converted to a lecture theatre, it was realised that the top half still existed in a storeroom above the theatre. Restoration then concentrated on the central panel, The Drama. The fragment was put on display at the official reopening of the People's Palace, after renovation. Alongside it, are displayed photographs of the building and murals from the venue's thirties heyday.

Bray's experience with the murals at the People's Palace was a forerunner to her collaboration over forty years as assistant to Hans Feibusch, a master of the medium. He oversaw projects at Chichester Cathedral, Dudley Town Hall in Worcestershire, the Civic Centre in Monmouth and many parish churches. Newport was a good example of the Feibusch and Bray collaboration, with her painting the landscape backdrops for his figure compositions. London examples were St Crispin's in Bermondsey, with a fine ceiling by Bray, and St Alban the Martyr in Holborn.

After her divorce from John Cooper, Bray married Eric Phillips, a distinguished civil servant. Bray was an energetic, athletic woman, who later in life would stride early in the morning to plunge at dawn into the ladies' pool near her home in Hampstead, turning a cartwheel on the Heath in celebration of her sixtieth birthday. But after suffering some years from Parkinson's Disease, she died on December 12, 1991.

David Buckman

The young Phyllis Bray

The story began one night long, long ago in a moonlit wood near the city of Athens. Through the green darkness under the trees a fairy came running and dancing. Suddenly she caught sight of a strange little creature with a twinkling merry face and stopped, perched on tiptoe. 'How now spirit, whither wander you?', called the stranger. She answered him in a song:

' Over hill, over dale
Thorough bush, thorough briar,
Over park, over pale,
Thorough flood, thorough fire,
I do wander everywhere
Swifter than the moones sphere.'

She told him her mistress, the fairy queen Titania, was coming that night to the woods with all her fairy courtiers. Then she looked again and recognised the little creature. It was Puck, who loved to get up to mischief frightening the village girls and whisking the stools from under old ladies, just as they were going to sit down. He was the favourite jester of Oberon, king of the fairies, and made his master smile with his wild pranks.

So Puck and the fairy talked about their master and mistress. There was trouble in fairyland. The king and queen had quarrelled over a little mortal boy. Titania stole him away from his father, an Indian king, and took him for her page. She crowned him with garlands of flowers and played with him by the hour. Oberon was jealous, he wanted the boy for himself to go hunting and tracking in the wild forests. And so they never met to dance in the moonlight…

'in grove or green,
By fountain clear or spangled starlight sheen.'

Instead they quarrelled till all their frightened elves crept into acorn cups to hide themselves.

Suddenly as Puck and the fairy were talking the wood was filled with sparkling light. From one side Titania with her fairy followers came threading through the moonbeams and from the other Oberon stepped into the glade to meet her:

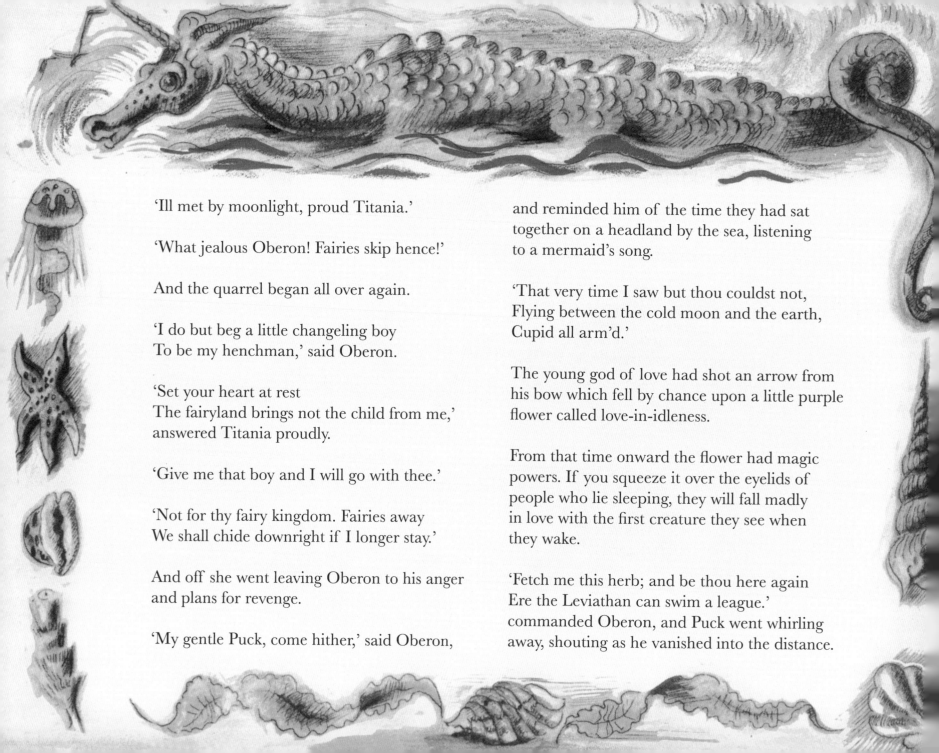

'Ill met by moonlight, proud Titania.'

'What jealous Oberon! Fairies skip hence!'

And the quarrel began all over again.

'I do but beg a little changeling boy
To be my henchman,' said Oberon.

'Set your heart at rest
The fairyland brings not the child from me,'
answered Titania proudly.

'Give me that boy and I will go with thee.'

'Not for thy fairy kingdom. Fairies away
We shall chide downright if I longer stay.'

And off she went leaving Oberon to his anger
and plans for revenge.

'My gentle Puck, come hither,' said Oberon,

and reminded him of the time they had sat
together on a headland by the sea, listening
to a mermaid's song.

'That very time I saw but thou couldst not,
Flying between the cold moon and the earth,
Cupid all arm'd.'

The young god of love had shot an arrow from
his bow which fell by chance upon a little purple
flower called love-in-idleness.

From that time onward the flower had magic
powers. If you squeeze it over the eyelids of
people who lie sleeping, they will fall madly
in love with the first creature they see when
they wake.

'Fetch me this herb; and be thou here again
Ere the Leviathan can swim a league.'
commanded Oberon, and Puck went whirling
away, shouting as he vanished into the distance.

'I'll put a girdle
            round about the earth in forty minutes!'

And Oberon went on thinking his thoughts:

            'Having once this juice,
I'll watch Titania when she is asleep
And drop the liquor of it in her eyes:
The next thing that she waking looks upon…
Be it lion, bear or wolf or bull
On meddling monkey or on busy ape…
She shall pursue it with the soul of love.
And ere I take this charm off from her sight,
As I can take it with another herb,
I'll make her render up her page to me.'

And as he thought he waited for Puck to come back with the flower.

In another part of the wood Titania was giving her fairies orders for the night and lying down to sleep. Her bed was a bank of wild thyme where oxlips and violets grew; a canopy of roses and honeysuckle hung over her head. She closed her eyes and the fairies sang her to sleep with a lullaby. First the queen's own fairy sang alone:

> 'You spotted snakes with double tongue
> Thorny hedgehogs be not seen,
> Newts and blindworms do no wrong,
> Come not near our fairy queen.'

Then softly they all sang the chorus together:

> 'Philomel, with melody,
> Sing in our sweet lullaby;
> Lulla, lulla, lullaby; lulla, lulla, lullaby;
> Never harm nor spell nor charm
> Come our lovely lady nigh.'

And as they sang the queen fell asleep. One by one the fairies slipped away between the trees and left her lying alone. She slept on.

Then out of the shadows, without a sound Oberon
came creeping. In his hand he held the little purple
flower that Puck had gathered for him. He bent
over her and watched her sleeping eyelids… then
slowly he squeezed the flower juice and whispered
the magic spell.

'What thou seest when thou dost wake,
Do it for thy true love take,
Love and languish for his sake.'

He left her lying under the power of the spell.
Everything was quiet in the green glade, only a
nightingale singing in the distance and the moon
riding high in the sky.

Suddenly there was noise of loud voices, footsteps and a jingling lantern. Five men came tramping into the glade, shouting at one another, falling over sticks and roots and rabbit holes. There was a little man with a squeaky voice… Flute the bellows mender; there was Snout the tinker, and Snug the joiner; there was an old wrinkled man for ever losing his spectacles, called Peter Quince, and last of all there was a fat, red, noisy man… Nick Bottom the weaver.

These five had come out from the city into the wood to rehearse a play they were soon going to act before the Duke of Athens on his wedding day. It was a wonderful play, as you could see when they began rehearsing. Fat Nick Bottom was the hero and squeaky Flute the heroine. Snug was a lion and rather worried about remembering his part, though as a matter of fact it wasn't difficult – it was all roaring.

Flute gabbled through all his speeches one after another without giving anyone else time to get a word in. None of them saw Puck perched in a tree watching them, hugging his sides with laughter, for already he thought of a way to make fools of them all. And all the time Queen Titania slept on, hidden under a canopy of flowers at one side of the glade.

Bottom went to hide behind a bush till it was his turn to speak, then he strutted out and cleared his throat ready to shout. At the sight of him, the others began to run away. They fell over one another and yelled with fright as they went. They shouted, 'Oh monstrous; Oh strange, we are haunted; Oh Bottom, thou art changed… help! help!'

Bottom had got a donkey's head! Puck had followed him into the bushes and bewitched him… just for fun. Bottom didn't understand what had happened. He stood there scratching his long hairy ears and wondering what to do. To cheer himself up he started to sing in his roaring voice. And at that moment Titania woke:

'What angel wakes me from my flowery bed?'

The magic spell had begun to work – she was falling in love with the fat man with a donkey's head.

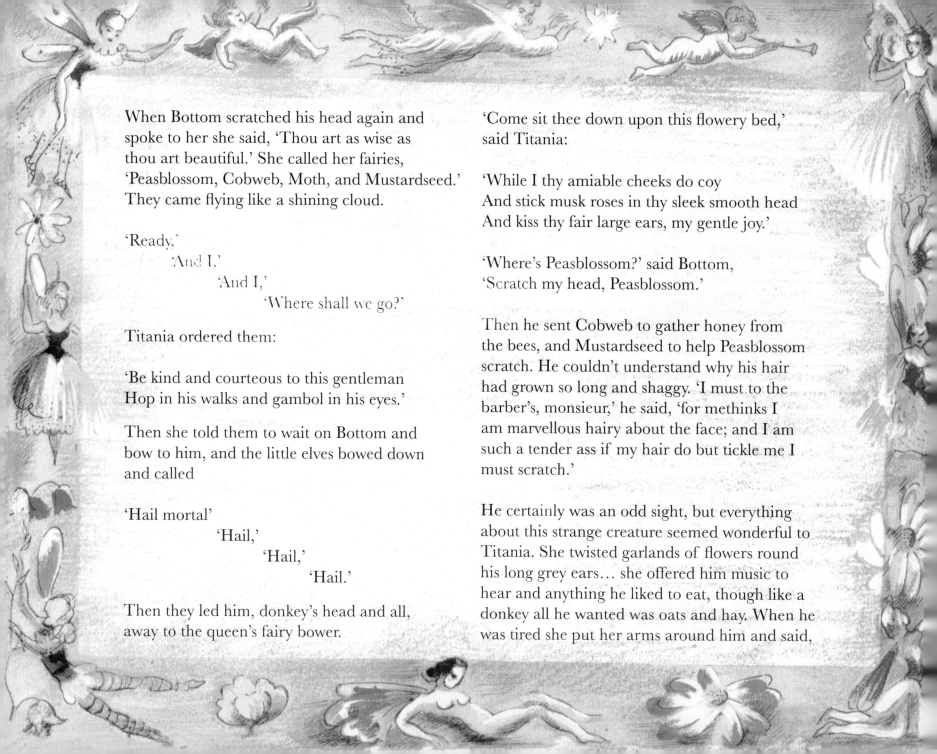

When Bottom scratched his head again and spoke to her she said, 'Thou art as wise as thou art beautiful.' She called her fairies, 'Peasblossom, Cobweb, Moth, and Mustardseed.' They came flying like a shining cloud.

'Ready,'
        'And I.'
                'And I,'
                        'Where shall we go?'

Titania ordered them:

'Be kind and courteous to this gentleman
Hop in his walks and gambol in his eyes.'

Then she told them to wait on Bottom and bow to him, and the little elves bowed down and called

'Hail mortal'
            'Hail,'
                    'Hail,'
                            'Hail.'

Then they led him, donkey's head and all, away to the queen's fairy bower.

'Come sit thee down upon this flowery bed,' said Titania:

'While I thy amiable cheeks do coy
And stick musk roses in thy sleek smooth head
And kiss thy fair large ears, my gentle joy.'

'Where's Peasblossom?' said Bottom,
'Scratch my head, Peasblossom.'

Then he sent Cobweb to gather honey from the bees, and Mustardseed to help Peasblossom scratch. He couldn't understand why his hair had grown so long and shaggy. 'I must to the barber's, monsieur,' he said, 'for methinks I am marvellous hairy about the face; and I am such a tender ass if my hair do but tickle me I must scratch.'

He certainly was an odd sight, but everything about this strange creature seemed wonderful to Titania. She twisted garlands of flowers round his long grey ears… she offered him music to hear and anything he liked to eat, though like a donkey all he wanted was oats and hay. When he was tired she put her arms around him and said,

'Sleep thou and I will wind thee in mine arms,' and she rocked him to sleep saying, 'Oh how I love thee, how I dote on thee.'

She forgot to quarrel with Oberon when they met, she even forgot the little Indian boy. When Oberon asked for the boy again she gave him up without a word, and sent her fairy flying with the child in her arms.

Now he had the page even Oberon began to feel sorry for poor Titania, in love with her donkey. So he sent Puck to find the other flower… the one that would undo the magic spell. Carrying the flower they crept to the queen's bower once again. Then they hid themselves behind a tree trunk and watched. They watched Titania as she lay sleeping with her arms twined round the donkey's shaggy neck.

Oberon turned to Puck and whispered:

'Seest thou this sweet sight?
Her dotage now I do begin to pity
And now I have the boy, I will undo
This hateful imperfection of her eyes.'

He took the flower and bending over
Titania he touched her eyes with it.

'Be as thou wast wont to be
See as thou wast wont to see.
Dian's bud o'er Cupid's flower
Hath such force and blessed power.
Now my Titania wake; you my sweet queen.'

Titania opened her eyes:

'My Oberon! What visions have I seen!
Methought I was enamoured of an ass.'

'There lies your love,' said Oberon pointing to

Bottom, who was snoring with his donkey mouth wide open and a garland of flowers slipping rakishly over one eye.

'How came these things to pass?' cried the poor fairy queen:

'Oh, how mine eyes do loath his visage now.'

And so the quarrel was made up. Oberon and Titania called fairy musicians to play and once again they danced together. Puck took the donkey's head off poor stupid Nick Bottom and left him still asleep on the ground with his own red face. The night passed merrily till Puck cried:

'Fairy king attend and mark
I do hear the morning lark.'

Then they flew away and all that was left of them was the sound of fairy music fading into the distance. That is really the end of the story of Oberon and Titania. But perhaps you would like to know that Bottom did get home safely and all his friends were very pleased to see him.

They did act their play in the palace before the Duke and Duchess and it was a great success… in a way. Everyone roared with laughter, although it was supposed to be very sad. After the play was over the actors, the Duke and Duchess and everyone else in the palace went to bed. Then Puck crept out with a little broom to sweep the floor before Oberon and Titania called their fairies out to dance in the Duke's great hall. First Oberon commanded them;

'Through this house give glimmering light,
By the dead and drowsy fire:
Every elf and fairy sprite
Hop as light as bird from brier.
And this ditty after me
Sing and dance it trippingly.'

Then Titania answered:

'Hand in hand with fairy grace
Will we sing and bless this place.'

They danced in and out of the patches of moonlight

on the marble floor, up the stairs, through the windows over the balconies and colonnades and over all the palace, while Oberon sang:

> 'Trip away
>   Make no stay
>   Meet me all by break of day.'

Then at the first light of morning they all vanished.